"*face-to-faces* is a book of 'moth bitten kisses,' a book about separation and connection. KRISTINE ESSER SLENTZ has written a remarkable hybrid collection which asks what is intimacy and where might we find it? From Feeld to a 'boyfriend list' to DMs and notes apps to QR codes, this book delights in its own form, just as it questions boundaries and old forms of love and marriage. I love this book for its clear-eyed examination of polyamory, just as I love its sheer playfulness and invention. KRISTINE ESSER SLENTZ has given us a text that surprises us at every turn, a collection that is 'more of a spell than any question.'"

—NICOLE COOLEY, author of *Mother Water Ash*, winner of The Walt Whitman Award from the Academy of American Poets, Discovery/The Nation Award, NEA, and the Emily Dickinson Award from the Poetry Society of America

"In *face-to-faces*, KRISTINE ESSER SLENTZ blurs the line between body and machine, longing and loss, to reveal how desire and power collide in the digital age. These poems move 'deep among brain folds,' pulsing with the electric strangeness of our mediated lives: 'download app / turn on song / turn on toy / record / send.' Here we are pressed against the truth of who we are and the world around us, returning to the urgent question: how do we love, even when fractured? With wit and incision, Kristine never pretends love is whole. She exposes the ache, the glitch, the silence between messages, where honesty becomes a form of intimacy, and where we are always, as one poem reminds us, 'instant / after—.' This is a document of vulnerability and survival, where poetry becomes both confession and resistance. *face-to-faces* is raw, intimate, and hauntingly human."

—KAY POEMA, *author of Diary of an Intercessor* and former Bronx Poet Emerita

"*face-to-faces* is a captivating archive of modern intimacy equal parts erotic ledger, grief-document and digital séance. KRISTINE ESSER SLENTZ writes from the charged epicenter of desire where sexts, therapy worksheets, polyamorous kink, and domestic survival collide on the same glowing screen as she maps the messy negotiations of autonomy and attachment with a lyric precision that cuts through shame and spectacle. *face-to-faces* is a real-time record of emotional labor, of connection and disconnection. Slentz is doing something totally new and unforgettable."
—SANDRA SIMONDS, Winner of the Reader's Choice Award from Academy of American Poets, Vermont Book Award in Fiction, & shortlisted for the Dzanc Fiction Prize

"'...make Me / feel I can be / on-demand...'
KRISTINE ESSER SLENTZ's apt, piercing poly-dimensional collection, *face-to-faces* grants readers access to a speaker inhabiting a streamed-like quarantine. Anchored during the COVID pandemic, a period in which technology brokered relationships with others, ourselves, and gadgetry itself, eventually migrating into post-virus/viral environments, *face-to-faces* offers a kind of facsimile of daily life and love. Esser Slentz's speaker asks, "What does an emotional [SIC] relationship look like between screens?" Filled with text and texts, QR Codes, and found written scraps, Esser Slentz employs her elegant, searing craft to immerse the reader/user in a revelatory unmasking, inviting us to consider our lives in quick response interactions. Mirrored perspective is replaced by a kind of URL existence, a site/sight with multiple landing pages, reflections and refractions. "i love being the other / woman so much / I made Myself / her in My marriage," Esser Slentz's speaker reveals. What is most striking is the humanity in these intimate pages: heartbreak, empathy, cayenne and brownies, lemons—despite—or perhaps because of—the new-world algorithms *face-to-faces* considers. A vital, stunning collection."
—H.E. FISHER, author of *Sterile Field*

face-to-faces slithers with inventive forms and hypnotic language that carry you through the highs and lows of love: virtual, blooming, encoded, public, and personal. As she turns from sensual and comforting to heart-wrenching and confessional, KRISTINE ESSER SLENTZ archives her longing and invites us in — what a gift from a blazing and experimental voice that defines this poetry generation."
—JOE NASTA, author of *(friendship poems)*

"Writing from depths of the pandemic, KRISTINE ESSER SLENTZ's *face-to-faces* searches unrelentingly for connection in a deeply fraught time. Navigating the messy process of making a You into a We alongside the unmaking and remaking of the I, Slentz' lyrics shrewdly employ lines left hanging and stanzas left suspended to echo the feeling in those days of things being surreal, then unreal, then tragically, all too real. Refreshingly ambivalent towards the many mediations of the modern age, Slentz here offers wordplay, erasures, and collage first as a response to trauma but also, surprisingly, a path through it. A courageous, biting collection: peroxide on the wound."
—BENJAMIN MORRIS, author of *The Singing River*

"*face-to-faces* isn't just a collection of poems; it's an inventive archive commemorating how we survive and flourish in the digital age. In verses brimming with winking romanticism and grit, Kristine Esser Slentz embraces the absurd without ever losing warmth, juxtaposing transcendent lyric gestures with an influencer's linguistic flair. This multimodal book is an act of joy and a song of delight for our times."
—SARA WALLACE, author of *The Rival*

"With language electric like a live wire post storm, KRISTINE ESSER SLENTZ's *face to faces* vividly maps out stories of broken boundaries, the embodied and disembodied woundings and joys of intimacy, the heights and lows of love, along with the unparalleled enrichments that flow from cultivating our own families of choice and languages of love, so that in the end we ultimately are able to name and claim the inner culinary of our own desires."
—JAMES DIAZ, author of *Once More, Into the Light*

face-to-faces

An archive of confinement,
catching feelings, cooking, &
polyamorous kink.

KRISTINE ESSER SLENTZ

Thirty West Publishing

Est. 2015

ISBN-13: 979-8-9987727-1-9
Cover artwork by Shannon Hozinec
Cover design by Josh Dale
Edited by Olivia Zarzycki
Author photo by Corey Ewing
First Edition: January 2026
Printed in the U.S.A.

For more titles and inquiries, please visit:
www.thirtywestph.com

Table of Contents

FIRST FRIEND REQUEST: RESULTED IN CEREMONIAL OF SACRED SPOUSE 12

INTRODUCTION 13

FRIDAY THE 13TH 14

COMMERCE TO CONFINEMENT/TO SOCIAL MOTION ... 17

SUB-SANDWICH IN SPACE, BABY 18

DEEP IN LOCKDOWN 22

LET'S MAKE A BOYFRIEND LIST 25

HE ADDED TO HIS STORIES 27

INTO THE DMS 28

TRUST 29

NOT A DM SLIDE BUT SIGHTSEEING 30

HE ASKED ME FOR 34

MY WORDS FOR HIM, DADDYX 34

PAST WORDS 35

NEW RELATIONSHIP(S) ENERGY 37

HOW DID YOU PITCH POLY TO YOUR WIFE? 38

TABLED 40

LITTLE MISS 41

VIOLATE VULNERABILITY 42

INTERNAL FILL: POLY EDITION 43

THE BREAKDOWN 45

CYCLE 48

YOU CHOOSE THIS SHOT 51

WORKSHEET 53

HUSBAND VS MARRIAGE THOUGHTS 55

TEXT MESSAGES 57

Table of Contents

TYPE OUT THE BOUNDARIES TO SET THE SCENE 58

BLUNDER OF THE BOX INSTRUCTIONS 59

DEAR ASTRAL PROJECTION I AM ABOUT

TO BREAK UP WITH: 62

TEXT MESSAGE: 67

LEAVE HIS MANHATTAN 69

ACKNOWLEDGMENTS...73

ABOUT THE AUTHOR..74

ABOUT THE PUBLISHER 76

face-to-faces

FIRST FRIEND REQUEST: RESULTED IN CEREMONIAL OF SACRED SPOUSE

late-night breakfasts waited up
time sliced to traded chairs
moth-bitten kisses broken cup
to share

hard-pressed counter sweats
and ∞ wishes barreled stare
teething silver-packed cigarettes
to share

with living destroyed luck bare
passed long-lasting rib
to share

certification of separation
unfollow : remove : blocked

INTRODUCTION
a poly presentation

My girlfriend and my husband
here's My husband's boyfriend
and this is his boyfriend's wife
now, meet her boyfriend
that's My husband's boyfriend's wife's boyfriend
that My girlfriend just met
who wants us to meet his best friend
because his best friend has only met his girlfriend
who's the wife of my husband's boyfriend
they grew up together
I met my husband on holiday years ago
while I met My girlfriend last year
when my husband's boyfriend and wife moved to the city
where she met her boyfriend on a dating app
basically, I'd like you to meet
My family

FRIDAY THE 13TH
Marriage + COVID Edition

incision derision
chlorine dream

marked masks
eat dark streets

the flu the virus the plague
march on ides preview

decision collision
sanitize surprise

global gloves
shit white paper

move to new
states of cyber

shelter in place
admin disgrace

look essential
home work

navigate novel
grief patterns

birds alarm
city sirens

kitchen cook or
parish at cum hand

the variants the vulnerable the valued
such strong sirens scream

I want

My body

include intimacy
ingredients listed

instructions for
individual to follow

learn to make
mistakes on

except for those
who already know

who prepared
on others' bodies

My body
I want

mastered chef

COMMERCE TO CONFINEMENT/TO SOCIAL MOTION

harlem's 330 sq feet
pinpoint unpleasant
grove street
fighter pilot
salary calculator
fraction simplified
blue pedal boat
pumps online
jobs firing off
freeze dried
mango salsa
gma's red recipe book
strike month-of-month
binge game numbers
thrones for sale

SUB-SANDWICH IN SPACE, BABY
—For those who met on Feeld when it was open worldwide, 2020 an Odyssey.

cakes for cats
meow remixes
trap measure

hit enter
sub space

meaning of *carnation*
flowers in the attic
exhaust fanned

hit enter
sub space

napkin holder
toothpaste squeezer
juice cleanse

hit enter
sub space

heal prayer
lit candle

hit enter
sub space

blue chip
and dale earnhardt jr
cheesecake factory

hit enter
sub space

reset apple
online store hours
too minutes in a year

hit enter
sub space

tighten rake snake
game night
stand mixer

hit enter
sub space

vodka sauce
pizza dough
donuts delivery

hit enter
sub space

19

food bazaar
magazine covers
letter of resignation

hit enter
sub space

sample size
chart of accounts
receivable turnover ratio

hit enter
sub space

test internet speed
of sound synonym
for authentic watches

hit enter
sub space

brands of tequila
sunrise time
in new York (for now)

hit enter
sub space

unemployment extension
cuts of cord blood

pressure cookers

hit enter
sub space

pot roast
potatoes on the grill
say, *shut the fuck up.*

DEEP IN LOCKDOWN

couched conversation
finger soft folds
establish cravings
cream fill confections
give instructions
check availability
of edible fixings
time to turn on
sense vibration
wait as evening
juices squeeze
sound exits device
predict to take pics
what angles bring
the most mouth-
wet pleasure

now, turn off
hand mixer

I want nets
of binges started
simultaneously
& wine
make Me
feel I can be
on-demand
never been
kissed
phoned taps sent

Since we're here alone
and have all this time
and my therapist thinks it's a good idea,

LET'S MAKE A BOYFRIEND LIST

- Good dick* and good morning texts*
  - ○ (Zoom therapist states this is from going un//noticed)
    Revisit the absence of past birthday cards

- Loves food that isn't just beige
  - ○ (Zoom therapist states this is from food scarcity//disorder)
    Revisit a local pantry now*

- Gives quality time
  - ○ (Zoom therapist states this is because my parents//)
    Revisit weekend visitations

- Encourages my talents
  - ○ (Zoom therapist states this is how I feel worth//validation*
    Revisit unpaid guitar lessons

- Respects boundaries
  - ○ (Zoom states I don't respect my own boundaries*)
    Revisit childhood journals, especially sparkly one

25

- Takes care of me – health/money
  - (I struggle // to take care ///// myself*)
    Revisit the first savings account from the pineapple bank
- Self-aware and continuing to grow
  - (Zoom says I am too self-aware ////// to grow*)
    Revisit therapy in another state

(Reader, if you've read this far, you know where this is going)

HE ADDED TO HIS STORIES

trauma response trauma response trauma response trauma response

My reply: I didn't know that.

I grew up petrified too.

trauma response trauma response trauma response trauma response

His: I knew that.

Let me show a share again

– it's kinked.

trauma response trauma response trauma response trauma response

INTO THE DMS

M: Same! Big piercing fan.

H: Lotus between shoulder blades,
hamsa on rib cage,
flowers along
chest and
over shoulders,
semicolon on inner wrist.

M: Didn't realize...

H: I like to hide surprises. LOL.

M: Haha – fair enough

H: How about You?

M: They all sound very... intriguing... ;-P

H: Oh, I missed a tattoo.
I have a   plague
doctor on arm

TRUST

tempt trust
      tip touch

over rush waiting
sprinkle bound
snack on bond
      break

  seek
  tell tracks last online
looped video
silent cries into speakers
      or maybe letters

create super charged barriers
who did You let go
down   more
    than

NOT A DM SLIDE BUT SIGHTSEEING

I think about what it would be like to be
locked down
with You in
an oddly shaped cul-de-sac
than cemented buildings

        middles of curated corn
        than crowds of cockroaches

        over skyway states
        than trained coast

I think about how I
don't want to be
thoughtful
        of Your
        or of My
        why

i love being the other
woman so much
I made Myself
her in My marriage

we are
instant

aftercare
following

bright flesh
or burns

recognize
Our

body
counts later

HE ASKED ME FOR
MY WORDS FOR HIM, DADDYX

Open notes app to complete His task of me. Begins:

Very good, xxx
Impressive, xxx
I love how you   do that
Gorgeous
Thank you, xxx
Thank you, xxx
Thank you, xxx
you're so good   at that
Delicious
Do it again
Excellent, xxx
Magnificent job, xxx
you're beautiful, xxx

Please don't ever say you're proud of me.

Some things should stay
in the notes app.

PAST WORDS

so then was it
written by hand
direct from dick
pics to epics
next to the goo
that crawls
between breasts
plate and float
ribs to bad swing
I am not a swinger
no matter how
much brown liquor
lime rocks under
ice when months felt
like more months
sure this is time too
break up the day
because it won't
ever feel good
or nice or together
instead of waiting
for fingernails
to disappear
and hair under
the bed

NEW RELATIONSHIP(S) ENERGY

bought & shipped electronic devices
Our many voices call out to
Your honorific and then Mine

over and over and over again in
separate homes and living rooms

Your domination doesn't stop
    download app
    turn on song
    turn on toy
    record
    send

think of thirsty videos
but what even matters
because a new one will
provide by mourning
stop morning

HOW DID YOU PITCH POLY TO YOUR WIFE?

Did You take her for a walk?
We talked about my filthy city walks in St. Nicolas Park and yours in your affluent Midwestern neighborhood when we couldn't see anyone else but only hear our voices. *We loved it.*

Did You tell her how we knew each other?
We met back in 2011 at work at tech startup. Coming off religion and recession was so weird then. *We loved it.*

Or how we started talking again?
We needed love. *We loved it.*

Better yet, *why* we started talking again?
We needed love. *We loved it.*

Did You tell her what You told Me?
Of course not. *We loved it.*

Did You tell her how she would not get between us?
Of course not. *We loved it.*

Will You tell her how it's different from swinging?
Of course not. *We loved it.*

Will You tell her You love Me?
Of course not. *We loved it.*

That this love might be tough – but we can always take a future trip to each other?
We loved it.

TABLED

finally spray paint project coffee table legs
press into area rug to wood floor
all of time – push of gravity
the way it always is
did You write it
or was it logged
deep among brain folds
how do we love warmly
warm under wet supports
like bright duvet covers and digital
stimulation produce places for comfort cocktails

LITTLE MISS

You-

        -don't- -{get to}- know

she said so

VIOLATE VULNERABILITY

did anything pass beyond
passwords – sorry codes
was the code unobtrusive
enough that construction
went unnoticed unseen by
everyday messages located
in place in box in hand
then was it written
by hand direct from
cock pics to poems
next to the goo that
crawls between My
breast plate & float
ribs to bad to swing
I am not a swinger
no matter how much
clear liquor I pull in
citrus with rocks under
ice when months sure
this is time to break
because it won't ever
feel good or together
instead wait for fingernails
disappear & hair under the bed

INTERNAL FILL: POLY EDITION

What does an emotional relationship look like between screens? Is kissing the extent of contact once we can have physical touch on each other's skin??//When are scheduled phone calls? <u>FOR HOW LONG</u>?//Where do midnight text messages fall in this?//Are there parameters around our date night out in My hometown?//How open is the made-up, undetermined label publicly?//WHEN would the overnight nap happen since it'll be less than eight hours? What would Your idea of consistent visits to my living space(s) look like?//Will you let Me know *Your* designated alone TIME is? Where do You stand on My play partners/sex sessions? Our first time having sex will be WHEN? How can I trust You again? How do I know your other partner(s) won't harm Me/Us again?

circle

(therapy   sexting)

talk

THE BREAKDOWN

You start Our session
on My nipples
on Your tongue
or flicking to lips
give Me a pro tip
to tech touch point
with remote controls

Your recognition
wasn't supposed to be
the beginning of Our health
yet – it becomes scheduled
– like all good poly activities
week after 3 months gone

how do You stay?
was it reading manipulation?

hours blocked behind beds too
yes, I guess I'll stay here now
but, did You create choice?
do I cite eye at surprise
us girls grab four calls
to cry at goings out here

midnight – witch for you

so We break(s)

We see friendly now
abandonment digs on Your
marriage date night deep
Your tricks eat pretty in parking lots
lights & socialization & polish
She is naked threats – though not

sure – once
measurements were made for Us
but when has that given Me
love to not reenact/react
petty pain on
predicted perception
every nine-inch long
Our middles of rotten
You, Me, We swallowed

CYCLE

roots unseen
        —are ok &
20/20 pounds and a few
kids in different state
        of unrest
I hear the problems because how
I've lived them
        – each one faint
between quick   rushes against muscles

cover phone
    will the trick door work?

did i post
that picture
on all My
social media
platforms so
You would
reach out
to Me please
care for Me
now because
You didn't care
enough for Me
before so I
left on read
but now
I virtually
beg You to
still care or
show that
You did to
begin with
is that it or
do I want
change like
I want
or are You
still married to
Your wife or
learned to be
emotionally

unabusive
with Yourself

YOU CHOOSE THIS SHOT

with reckless thumbs
uninteresting tongue
and packed pancreas

stole My published secrets
watched left before You so
her groups of conversation
promises stamped I sealed

how many recommendations
or book-making can be made
until I wriggle out this rented
beds or public transportation

check the hour against
a weekday or guideline
wait with wine and ink
two months to may be

meanwhile My spouse giggles
thru phones to stumble more
in love tightens bunny's rope
we all ran across country too

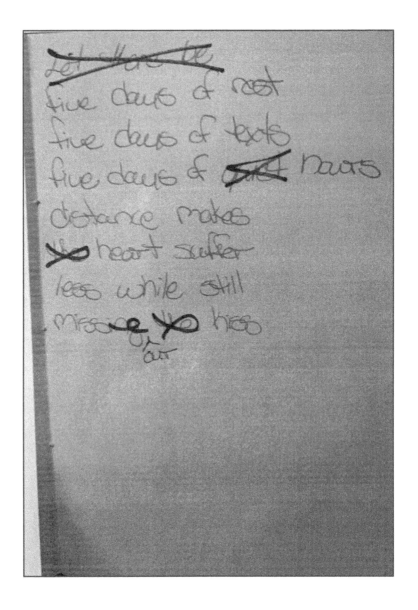

~~Let there be~~
five days of rest
five days of ~~texts~~
five days of ~~just~~ hours
distance makes
~~the~~ heart suffer
less while still
missing ~~the~~ his
air

WORKSHEET

In therapy and times of crisis, sometimes worksheets can help. Complete the questions below.*

What's going toward transformation?
What's the long-term plan now that we will live?
How will I know these new rules will be kept in place?

*Who will die now?

(drunk writing)
((i distaste you))

3 to be
people of the a.m.
specifically to be
sliced out
isolation and now
I am
here to declare
I wish
to be left so You
and Your living
addiction can wonder off
into My no-mans-land

go gobble shit and expire
I say see how it is
when we actually see each
other face-to-faces in allies
in broad ripples or in
a shaky dicks enter
or something like that ok
I feel sticky
give Me tomorrow
tonight You fucked

HUSBAND VS MARRIAGE THOUGHTS
– after Rosebud Ben-Oni

mars is in retrograde
and the air is cold
I close the bedroom
door that now rattles
it sounds like it will
open by someone strange
but that's just the pressure
from leaving the window open
I would've closed
the door if it wasn't
for the cats jumping
on my injured leg and
ankle curled up under
the clean duvet with
other hurt that suggests
I should message boys
in their late 20s & 30s
at 3 a.m. on a Tuesday
but pride or learning
self-worth is making
me perform otherwise
I think that maybe
masturbation will help
but orgasms never do
unless intention is applied
thanks and take that

to mean whatever
You'd like it to be
nothing is real anyways
as the stars say, *we
are all in a simulation*

TEXT MESSAGES

We can speak while. We can work this out while. We can change while.

M: Are You still leaving going to Nashville? ~~So You won't be here for my Leo birthday?~~

H: Yes ~~I cannot say no to everyone but You~~

M: Then no. ~~I am so angry and scared to set this boundary. I knew you would do this and this is why I am here.~~

H: Wow. ~~I really thought I could talk You into anything~~.

M: I've already expressed how I feel about being contacted during that time and why. I'm not going to put Myself in an emotionally harmful situation to make anyone feel better – especially after being so deeply hurt. That's it. ~~Relief. For now.~~

We can speak while. We can work this out while. We can change while.

57

TYPE OUT THE BOUNDARIES TO SET THE SCENE

damp tissue
old muscles
moist ropes
crave wound
blood scars
bite out the —
~~eaten alive~~

BLUNDER OF THE BOX INSTRUCTIONS

that feeling
Your face
feels after
crying in
Your sleep
lasts

boxed brownies
with extra
cinnamon and
cayenne pepper
and chocolate
chips bake
without sodium
add anger

how many
ways can I
say stop
speaking
because I
miss You

bodily memories   & hold
or phone calls — it was 20 minutes in and I
learned of an ending marriage by of force
and money on old types because we're all
criminals outside of Queens, right? Teach
them our ways   coded messages no one
reads but other breakers working against
constructed time or motion — eat bread

DEAR ASTRAL PROJECTION I AM ABOUT TO BREAK UP WITH:

Wake at witching hour.

You listed
what I needed
altered by other men
than You
other defenses
Is this what cursed looks like? I forget because of what the
guardians say.

are You prepared for Me
to test Your uncleansed childhood ritual
am I living My uncleansed childhood ritual

My asking
is symptom-proof
instead I strike a wick
I make sure it's not black or white wax. I hate red now.

why I ask You for personal protection
why don't I ask Myself
Incense would've been better.

More of a spell than any question.

call to find
what *she*
suggested
Nashville
a fertility
vacation
You felt
great way
to thank *her*
for *her* sacrifice
for Your
spent time
with Me
to show
Me love
depart for
six days
return on
My birthday
back in NYC
she is thankful for Nashville
she is thankful for My tears
she is thankful You didn't

do something
make Yourself

happy

sunflower field
take a picture
of Your wife's
back as she
photographs seeds
that will fall
to the ground soon

My husband is
making rose water
from the bouquet
You bought Me

We will make
something from this.

TEXT MESSAGE:

Please do not talk
to Me about dehumanizing
feelings. Since the work
started to try to be
a secondary partner
to You I felt like
no matter how much
we talked, processed, or
what have You —
I was stuck feeling
like I was ultimately
viewed as a less than.
**Spending time with Me
should never be someone's
sacrifice they deserve
a reward for.
— ever.**

LEAVE HIS MANHATTAN

apartment and walk 12
cement blocks to touch
Her lips on refined things
sand, liquid poison, rocks

She will sit there

trying to escape love but
two shots and lemon sucks
who knew with light flashes
regardless if snot stains
regardless if gin stains
lets talk about the wet bar
endless pieces of vapor
how nothing has real taste
but isn't what all of this is
something we've created to
fit or maybe to fix money
to power we don't have
sucking on this lime or
eat more to keep them happy
yes, the lie has more or less

happiness

there's still salt on My face
makeup missing from My chin

I'll look away at some point
thank Jim for the late love
served up and then to the left
by the to-go orders and fees

that's when
I realize My
favorite colors
are the shades
of a healing bruise

ACKNOWLEDGMENTS

The following works have been previously published and featured in these journals, anthologies, books, and magazines:

Five Points: "New Relationship Energy"
Promethean Magazine: "I Want My Body" and "Not a DM Slide but Sightseeing"
Anti-Heroin Chic: "cycle" and "worksheet"
Fever of the Mind: "type of the boundaries to set the scene," "Since we're here alone and have all this time and my therapist thinks it's a good idea, Let's Make a Boyfriend List," and "here we are"
Querencia Press: "Quarantine, baby" and "blunder of the box instructions"
Beyond the Veil: "do something" and "internal fill"
Queen Mobs Tea House: "ceremonial of sacred spouse"
The Shallow Ends: "introduction"
Stone Pacific Zine: collage pieces, audio (QR codes), "of me," "that's all"
4'33: "Deep in Lockdown"
(Re) An Ideas: "past words" and "Text Message"

ABOUT THE AUTHOR

Author Photo by Corey Ewing

KRISTINE ESSER SLENTZ is a queer writer of Maltese descent, raised in the Chicagoland area. A cult escapee and GED holder, she is the author of *EXHIBIT: an amended woman, depose* (FlowerSong Press, 2021, 2024) and *face-to-faces* (Thirty West Publishing House, 2026). She is a *TEDx* participant and regular contributor to *The Saturday Evening Post*. KRISTINE is the co-founder, organizer, and host of Adverse Abstraction, a monthly experimental artist series in New York City's East Village. She also produces and performs in *Verse & Vision*, a stage production currently in a micro-residency at NYC's DADA with consecutive runs at the IndyFringe Festival. Follow her art on Substack at *Carnations & Car Crashes*.

ABOUT THE PUBLISHER

Escape the Mundane | Est. 2015 in Pennsylvania

Follow us on:

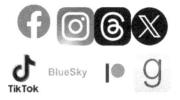

Scan the QR code to visit: `

www.thirtywestph.com